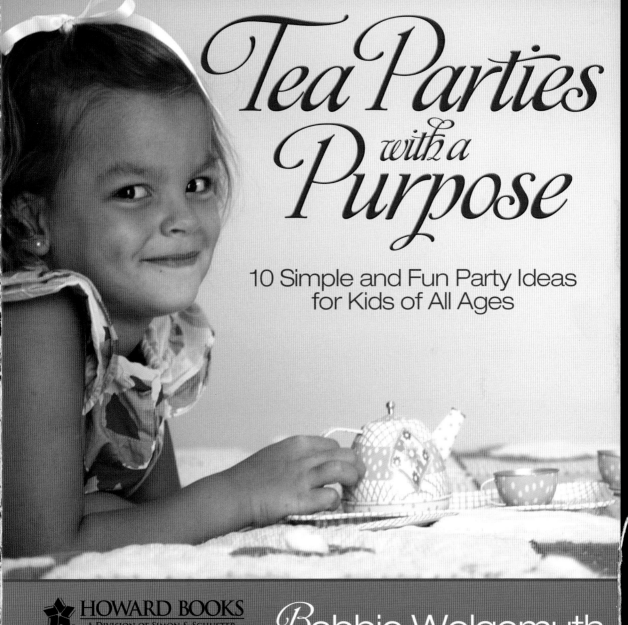

Tea Parties with a Purpose

10 Simple and Fun Party Ideas for Kids of All Ages

HOWARD BOOKS
A DIVISION OF SIMON & SCHUSTER
New York   London   Toronto   Sydney

Bobbie Wolgemuth

Our purpose at Howard Books is to:
Increase faith in the hearts of growing Christians
Inspire holiness in the lives of believers
Instill hope in the hearts of struggling people everywhere
Because He's coming again!

Published by Howard Books, a division of Simon & Schuster, Inc.
1230 Avenue of the Americas, New York, NY 10020
www.howardpublishing.com

HOWARD
BOOKS

Tea Parties with a Purpose © 2008 by Bobbie Wolgemuth

Library of Congress Cataloging-in-Publication Data
Wolgemuth, Bobbie.
  Tea parties with a purpose : 10 simple and fun party ideas for kids of all ages / Bobbie Wolgemuth.
     p.   cm.
1. Afternoon teas. 2. Children's parties. 3. Christian life. I. Title.
  TX736.W65 2008
  642—dc22   2008015962

ISBN-13: 978-1-4165-7294-7
ISBN-10:   1-4165-7294-5

10 9 8 7 6 5 4 3 2 1

Manufactured in China

For information regarding special discounts for bulk purchases, please contact: Simon & Schuster Special Sales at 1-800-456-6798 or business@simonandschuster.com.

Edited by Chrys Howard
Cover and interior design by Stephanie D. Walker
Photography by Julie Tassy, www.myzoomphotography.com, 2008

To Abby, Luke, Isaac, Harper, and Ella.
You make Nanny smile every day
and your joy spills over into every life you touch.

And to their mothers, Missy and Julie,
who faithfully prayed, planned, and celebrated
each tea party as if you were kids again.

I love you with all my heart.

Contents

Acknowledgments

Many thanks to the creative children and moms who offered their bright smiles and winsome personalities in the making of this book. Your delight took the fun to a whole new level.

Abby Schrader
Luke Schrader
Isaac Schrader

Harper Tassy
Ella Tassy

Grace Noble
Ian Noble
Rowan Noble
Allie Mowbray
Annabelle Mowbray

Taylor Burch
Claire Burch

Lois Wooden
Kylie Wooden
Bryce Wooden

Cyndi Hall
Abigail Hall
Margaret Hall
Thomas Hall

Lilly Cascio

Lillie Shanahan

Introduction

Tea Parties and Dreams

Dreams have the magical ability to take us to places we often don't get to go. While many dreams wake us in the night, some of our dreams are visions that distract us while we're wide awake. We call those daydreams. I have been blessed to have a recurring daydream that energizes and inspires me.

In my dream, I visualize two children who live near me sitting on the porch wasting away the hours. One is a little boy, the other a little girl. For lack of anything better to do, I can hear them picking on each other. As they see me walking toward them, their faces light up. "Miss Bobbie, is it time for another tea party?" the little girl is quick to ask. Smiling back at the two of them, I reply, "Yes, it is. Go ask your mom if you can come over. Tell her it will just take about thirty minutes." The little girl runs in the house and I turn my attention to her brother, who pretends to be too cool for a tea party. "You're welcome to come," I say. Soon we're on our way to sharing thirty minutes of eating, singing, making crafts, and reading.

This dream has become a reality for me many times over as I have welcomed neighbors, church friends, and, now, my own precious grandchildren into my home for tea parties that have a purpose. My pantry is stocked with the makings of many different parties—from teddy bears to ocean friends. All it takes is a little food, plain paper, some crayons, a few books, and lots of love.

"But," you say, "is a tea party powerful enough to have any lasting impact? Can a young child really get my message?"

Armed with the simple ideas in this book and just thirty minutes, you can help the children in your life transcend an ordinary day into a spectacular event. You can take them to places they need to go but may not find on their own. It may involve a half hour of your time, but the impact of those thirty minutes will fill their hearts with a curiosity for learning and a hope for tomorrow.

Remember this: Heaven can open the heart of a child in a split second of time. And when the Lord Jesus celebrates with a child, it counts for eternity.

Now, go out and make a difference in the life of a child and have fun while you do it!

How to Use This Book

Celebrations are important to children. Whether it's Christmas, a birthday, or a school field trip, as soon as the big day has come and gone, little ones start anticipating the next big event. But there's no reason to wait for birthdays and holidays to celebrate. With some creativity and a few household treats, you can make a children's tea party a special occasion any day. The way I see it is this, "If you announce it, they will come!" All you need is a fun theme, a (no-bake) snack, some colorful markers, a few sheets of paper, a good story, and a sweet smile. Your party is sure to be an event that is fun-filled and memorable. The best part is that when you host a simple party with enough excitement to entertain little guests, you can relax and enjoy it yourself. And when the kids beg for another party, you'll want to do it again.

Every Child Can Help

As you begin your tea party journey, you may want to include your own children or some children close to you in the preplanning. Part of the magic of a successful tea party comes from seeing children become excited about the upcoming event and letting them use their imaginations in the theme selection, preparation, presentation, and food creations. As you host more and more parties, your pantry will be stocked with the different theme items just as my pantry is. You will be able to use the same books and decorations over and over again.

As a starting point, let your children select a tea party theme from this book. The parties in this book are easy-to-follow, start-to-finish models for you and your guests to use. All of these themes require as much—or as little—imagination as you have; none have expensive or exorbitant trappings. If you let the kids browse these pages, they'll come up with the party that strikes their fancy and the planning begins. Selecting a party theme such as Teddy Bears, Under the Sea, Honeybees, or Angels creates a unified and bigger-than-life impression.

Take the children to your pantry as you look for products that you already have on hand. You will be amazed at how they will be able to find items to fit the theme that you didn't even see. Let them carry this book with them on the next trip to the grocery store. They will enthusiastically get involved in the shopping as they drop a few inexpensive treats into the cart that will help them complete their chosen tea party theme.

Every Child Needs a Hug

Once you have collected the necessary items, you're ready for the big event. Always begin the party with a hug, kind words, and eye contact. This is so important and can be easily overlooked by busy adults. Getting down on your knees so you can give an "arms wrapped around you" hug will be long remembered. Always notice something specific about each child and make them aware just how happy you are to be with them. A child feels cherished with the smallest encouragement. "You have such a happy smile today, you must be excited," or "That is such a cute toy you brought along. I can't wait for you to tell me about it," or "I like that bright flower on your shirt. You are like a burst of sunshine today." Remember your own childhood and the adults who made you feel wonderful with simple expressions of care. You have the ability to pass that kind of special attention on to a little person in your world.

Every Child Is an Artist

Even if you don't consider yourself an artist, the children in your life are. You can let them help you prepare the name tags and the party announcements ahead of time. It's important for children to realize that they cannot ruin anything. This is not an art contest; it's a fun expression of their talent. Your words of encouragement will help even the youngest child enjoy and participate in the preparation and the party. Before the party begins, set the tone by displaying some of the suggested objects, centerpieces, art pictures, books, cards, and toys. Seeing these items will give the party artists something to imitate or prime the pump for their own creation. As little hands progress on the crafts, give words of encouragement such as, "Tell me about your picture," or "I like the way you decided to decorate your fish." Let the child happily describe his purple fish or lime green house. Remember, the idea is to get the children to create their work in a comfortable, nonthreatening setting. There are no wrong answers or bad pictures. Their creation is an expression of the heart of the young artistic thinker. Each party has more than one craft idea. Just do what you have time to do.

Every Child Has a Voice

Recently, I was told that one of the most important indicators of business success among executives is the ability to comfortably and effectively make a presentation. One CEO said his earliest presentation memory was as a young boy when his mother sat in a chair and listened to his speeches. She was his only audience, but he says she contributed to his ability to grow into public speaking comfortably and successfully. I cannot overemphasize the benefits of allowing children to make tiny presentations to their friends and "audience of mom" on a regular basis.

This is one of my favorite parts of the tea party. I call it the "robin and the worm" theory of teaching social competence and speaking skills to children. The tiniest bit of warm success at making a presentation will encourage the child to dig deeper to unearth things that will produce greater success and feelings of self-confidence. The youngest child can safely hold her cherished teddy on her lap and tell her friends something about her bear, describe her favorite fruit, or show her drawing to the other tea party attendees.

Give every child a chance to "show and tell" to the group. I guarantee it will be a bigger deal than you can imagine. (Maybe someday a successful CEO or PTA moderator will stand and say, "It was at a tea party that I learned the art of public speaking.")

Every Child Has a Purpose

One way you can pass along the values you cherish is to share them through activities that children love to do. The arts and crafts that you do will teach children that God has given them a talent and to use that talent for Him. The food items will show children that nutritious snacks can be fun, too. This next part of the tea party may be my favorite. Children love to read, and books can become valuable friends to them. Books take us on excursions to places we would love to visit, but might never get to go to, and they allow us to meet people we might never get to meet. Books also teach us valuable life lessons in a friendly, nonthreatening way. That's why every tea party has a suggested book list to give you a starting place and let you know what is available. You should be able to find these books at your local library if you do not own them already.

Reading to children involves creating an exciting experience on the spot. They will understand how others think and feel and they can sift through lots of interesting information. Read stories you enjoy yourself. When you read aloud, ham it up and keep it lively so that the children are pulled along to play with the idea, trying it on physically and emotionally and artfully. If you're reading a book about a fish, stop and let everyone make fish faces. A good storyteller delights the children while noticing what the children like and what's working. You enthusiastically enter their world, drawing closer and closer to each other. And that's the connection you want. It's your reward and their blessing. Each tea party also includes a scripture and an application. Sharing valuable life lessons will give children the tools they need to succeed in life.

And Finally, Every Child Will Want to Come Back

When it's time to end the party, your favorite comment will probably come from one of the young people with whom you spent the last thirty minutes. As you smile and hug good-bye, they'll probably say, "That was fun! When can we have another tea party?"

Last week, I called my husband and told him, "We did a Hands and Feet tea party and I read a story about a raccoon and I got to be the mommy raccoon who kissed her baby's hand before he went to school." After a pause, he said, "Sounds like fun. Who are these parties really for, you or the kids?"

That's a good question.

With every party, I'm delighted to see the faces of children light up. And I enjoy my own excursion into their world for a brief time. Although each party is different, in every one we dream of things we can't see. We enjoy making friends through new experiences. All of this is done in the context of noticing God's creativity. It has been said, "What comes to our minds when we think about God is the most important thing about us." That's because our image of God shapes everything. It is forged when we think about His love and His truth, His design and His handiwork. It is with this in mind that I gently allow the children to be exposed to the image of God in everything we observe. From honeybees to hands and feet, we notice things in the world which have been designed for our good and God's glory. So, together with the children, we can expand our vision of the Heavenly Father, the living God. We are inviting Him to shape our spiritual futures while doing something right now . . . something as engaging and wonderful as having a tea party.

Welcome to the fun.

Bobbie Wolgemuth
Orlando, Florida

**Please join me for
Under the Sea
Tea!**
Be sure to
wear your
beachwear
and flip-flops!

Time:
Place:

Under the Sea Tea

Setting the Scene

- You can make a child swim with delight if you purchase a real goldfish and fishbowl at the store for around five dollars. It's a lively mascot for your Under the Sea Tea. If the parents of your guests are willing, one child could take the fish home as a door prize. Or you can keep it for young guests to enjoy on future visits.

- If you have any seashells stored from a past beach trip, add them around the table for a touch of the seashore.

- Have a deck of Go Fish cards ready for the beachcombers to enjoy.

- Make a sea by draping a large blue blanket, sheet, or tablecloth over two chairs. A blue towel on the floor will complete the underwater fort where all swimmers gather. Your guests will happily want to "dive" under the sea to begin your tea party.

- Dress in beachwear, complete with sunglasses or goggles.

Welcome

Greet each child as they enter with "I'm so glad you're here. Just swim right on in to our tea party. You are special to me! Are you ready to go to the seashore?"

Sea Menu

You don't have to use all of these ideas, but there are plenty here for you to choose from. Kids love them all! Some of these you will want to do ahead of time, others can be part of the party activities.

A Cute Crabby

- Slice a piece of apple to create a circular body for the edible crab.

- Place three cashews on each side to make the crab legs.

- Add round chocolate-covered peanut candies for the eyes. If you are concerned about serving peanuts, just use small chocolate chips.

Children will love to pick him apart when it's snack time!

Fishy Mix

Combine Goldfish crackers, pretzels, cereal pieces, and gummy fish-shaped fruit snacks for a favorite pick-up treat. Just the Goldfish will work if you don't want to add the rest.

Banoctopus

- Cut the stem off the end of a banana and peel it halfway down. Make sure to cut the peel into eight "legs."

- Break off half of the fruit that is inside the peeled part.

- Turn the unpeeled portion upside down on a plate to steady your octopus.

- Spread out the peel to look like legs.

- Draw two eyes with a marker on the face of the octopus.

- He will sit quietly on your tea table and watch the fun until snack time.

Sea Bubbles and Sea Foam Fun Drink

Here are a few suggestions for three different sea-foamy drinks.

- Serve lemon-lime soda—or anything with fizzy bubbles.

- Pour a bit of dark soda over a scoop of vanilla ice cream.

- Put any type of sherbet in a punch bowl and pour half ginger ale and half lemon-lime soda on top. Then serve the bubbly punch to your guests.

Story Time

Pick one, two, or all three of these great books.

Swimmy by Leo Lionni—A small black fish and his friends work together to escape danger in the sea.

A House for Hermit Crab by Eric Carle—A hermit crab makes many new friends who make his home colorful and beautiful.

About Fish by Cathryn Sill—A simple fish fact book with inspiring watercolor illustrations.

Express Yourself Time

Did you know that fish travel in groups called schools? That's why they are so smart! What do you like about school?

Can you tell me some words from the ocean or sea that start with *S*? (*Scales, scallops, swim, storm, stripes, spines, sea horse, snapping turtle, stingray, shark, seaweed, starfish, seacoast, seashells, sand*)

Do you know what a tongue twister is? A tongue twister is a group of words that is hard to say together, especially to say fast. See if you can say this one: "Susie sells seashells down by the seashore" three times fast.

Learning Time

Fish breathe through gills in their bodies. The gills take the oxygen the fish needs from the water in the sea. How do you breathe? Have you ever held your breath underwater?

Most fish lay eggs. But a male sea horse holds the babies in a pouch on his belly. When the little sea horses hatch, they pop out of the pouch and swim away. What other animals have pouches? (*Kangaroos*) What other animals lay eggs? (*Birds*)

Many fish have something special that protects them from their enemies. They may have colored scales that help them blend into their surroundings. They may have spines that would make an enemy afraid. God may have given them some other type of marking to hide them in the water and protect them.

Craft Time

Hermit Crab House

After reading *A House for Hermit Crab,* make a house for a hermit crab by drawing a spiral design on a paper plate. Glue any decorations you can gather to your house: pieces of cut paper or ripped tissue paper, sequins, stickers, buttons, or pom-poms.

Or create an edible crab by decorating your paper-plate shell with food items such as raisins, cereal, pretzels, gummy fish, small candies, or chocolate chips. They will stick to the shell with peanut butter or ready-made cake icing.

Fish Fun

With construction paper and crayons or markers and using the templates in the back of this book, decorate simple fish and starfish to put into your sea. You will need to have your fish shapes cut out ahead of time. Give the fish eyes, fins, scales, or special decorations.

Crackers for Swimmy

After looking at the pictures in the book *Swimmy*, you can make one big fish like Swimmy or his friends. Arrange Goldfish crackers on a large platter or cookie sheet in the shape of a large fish. Make Swimmy's eye with a raisin or chocolate-covered peanut.

Lesson Time

One day as Jesus was standing by the Lake of Gennesaret, with the people crowding around him and listening to the word of God, he saw at the water's edge two boats left there by the fishermen who were washing their nets. He got into one of the boats, the one belonging to Simon, and asked him to put out a little from shore. Then he sat down and taught the people from the boat. When he had finished speaking, he said to Simon, "Put out into deep water, and let down the nets for a catch." Simon answered, "Master, we've worked hard all night and haven't caught anything. But because you say so, I will let down the nets." When they had done so, they caught such a large number of fish that their nets began to break. So they signaled their partners in the other boat to come and help them, and they came and filled both boats so full that they began to sink.
—Luke 5:1–7

Application

Jesus' friends were discouraged because they had been fishing all night and hadn't caught anything. Jesus told them to go back out onto the lake one more time and throw out their fishing nets. They had been trying and trying. I'm sure they were

tired. But they obeyed Jesus. Do you see what happened? *When the fishermen did as Jesus told them, they caught so many fish that the nets began to break.* Jesus provided what they needed ... and much more. He helps you and me when we obey, too. God loves you and knows what you need. Is there anything that seems too difficult for you that you would like us to pray about?

Prayer Time

Thank you, Lord, for our fun time under the sea with my special friends. You made so many beautiful fish and delightful creatures in the sea. You take care of them. Thank you for taking good care of me, too. You are a good and generous God. Amen.

Little drops of water,

little grains of sand,

God made the deep blue ocean

with His mighty hand.

Tea Today
All Flakes Welcome

**Please join me for a
Snowflake Tea Party!**

Snuggle up in a T-shirt, warm sweater,
or just a hat and gloves.

Time:

Place:

Snowflake Tea Party

Setting the Scene

- Set the table with a dark-colored tablecloth.

- Cover the dark cloth with lacy doilies that look like snowflakes. Your guests will make some more later in the party.

- Use white cups, plates, and napkins.

- Use some string and hang a few doily snowflakes directly over the table.

- Put a white sheet around the base of the table to look like snow.

- Have plenty of white paper, paper doilies, small child-safe scissors, pens, and crayons available in a basket.

- Mittens, gloves, or a snow globe add a festive touch to the table along with little marshmallow snowmen.

Welcome

Greet each child as they enter and say, "Come on in for a snowy good time." As you walk to the table you can sing, "When the weather outside is frightful, our tea will be delightful. And since we've no place to go, let it snow, let it snow, let it snow!" All flakes welcome. Whether it's hot or cold outside, we can have a snowflake party any time of year. We can celebrate snow on a hot summer day and make crafts to save for Christmas.

Snowy Day Menu

Snow-Dusted Cookies

Chocolate or vanilla slice-and-bake cookies work great for this snow-covered delight. Have the cookies ready when the children arrive, and let them dust powdered sugar on top. Place a doily on top of the cookie and let the children sprinkle the powdered sugar on it. Lift the doily for a pretty surprise.

If you have a snowflake or star cookie cutter, press it into a soft cookie to make the shape, and sprinkle it with powdered sugar to create a lacy design.

Mini Carrot Snowman Treat

Serve this healthy treat that is often used for the nose of a snowman.

Frosty Desserts

Snow cones, ice cream, or Popsicles are always a treat whether the day is hot or cold.

Warm Your Tummy Winter Drink

Serve hot chocolate with mini marshmallows on top to warm your guests on a chilly day.

Icy Icicle Tea

Place ice cubes in an ice bucket and let the children add their own ice to any drink you choose to serve. Tongs work great for picking up ice.

Craft Time

Paper Snowflakes

- Fold thin white paper in half, and in half again.

- Round the corners to form a circle and notch the paper with several V-shaped cuts. For small children, you might need to mark the cutouts before you let them cut. If they are too young to cut, let them mark where the cuts go and let older children or adults help with the cutting.

- Let each child unfold the snowflake and discover the pattern.

- Add the snowflakes to your table for decorations or hang some from the chandelier or ceiling.

- Round or square doilies make elegant snowflakes when you fold them and make some cuts in the center section or notch the outer edges slightly.

Marshmallow Snowmen

- Stack three large marshmallows on top of one another. Place the first one on a plate, and then cut the ends off the other two so they will stick together.

- Cut a raisin in half and push the sticky side into the snowman's face for the eyes.

- Arms are made of a pretzel stick broken in half and pushed into the middle marshmallow.

- A walnut or chocolate peanut butter cup can be set on his head for a cute (and yummy) hat.

Story Time

Pick one, two, or all of these great books.

Dream Snow by Eric Carle—A fun story about a farmer, his animals, and a snowstorm.

Footprints in the Snow by Cynthia Benjamin—An easy reader about animals finding their way home in the snow.

The Bravest Dog Ever: The True Story of Balto by Natalie Standiford—A wonderful story about a dog who travels many miles through the snow to get medicine to save sick children.

The Snowman by Raymond Briggs—A sweet textless book about a boy and his snowman, who comes to life.

Express Yourself Time

Did you know that no two snowflakes are alike? It's hard to believe that out of all the snowflakes God makes, no two are the same. Just like people. Even identical twins are not exactly alike. Sometimes you might not be able to tell twins apart, but their mothers always can because she sees little differences. God made only one of you. You are very special. Let's look at the snowflakes we all made. Do you see that no two are alike? Now let's look around the room and notice that we are all unique and each person is very special.

   Is there something nice you would like to say about the person sitting next to you? Your words can float out of your mouth like a pretty snowflake and make someone feel good. If you wish, you may also say something that is good about yourself. I'll start. (Examples: "I notice that Katy is as sparkling as the bow in her hair," or "I like Sam's happy eyes," or "Today Lillie's smile is extra bright," or "I can tell that Luke is artistic by the way he enjoyed making that snowflake.")

Lesson Time

As the rain and the snow come down from heaven . . .
so is my word that goes out from my mouth . . . It will . . . accomplish
what I desire and achieve the purpose for which I sent it.
—Isaiah 55:10–11

Children are like
snowflakes . . .
no two are exactly alike.

Application

The Bible says that God sends the snow down for a special reason. He uses snow to water the ground and make things grow. And the words in the Bible are like snow and rain that come down to make us grow. We want good words to fall on us so we grow to be happy and strong. That's why we read the Bible.

Prayer Time

Lord, thank you for snow. You made each of us special and unique like snowflakes. Thank you for my friends. Amen.

Honeybee Tea

Setting the Scene

- A bright tablecloth or place mats or napkins with a flower or fruit design will work great for this theme. Just use what you have around the house.

- Arrange a fruit centerpiece using any fruit available (to be used later in craft time).

- A honey jar can be part of the display (try to find one with a honeycomb inside).

- Lay out some yellow, white, and black paper and markers for pictures and notes.

- Any flowered teacups and a teapot or pitcher with a fruit or flower design completes the setting.

- You'll need a small basket or bowl to be the "honeycomb" for the "sweet word" game during lesson time.

Welcome

Greet each child as they enter and say, "I'm so glad you're able to *bee* here today. Buzz right on in to the party. We have so much to do and learn today. It will be a *bee*-u-ti-ful day!"

Bee Menu

You don't have to use all of these ideas, but there are plenty here for you to choose from. Kids love them all!

Honey Grahams

For a quick and easy treat, you can simply pass out honey graham crackers (they even come in bumblebee shapes).

Honey Toast

If you have a toaster, let the kids make their own toast. After it pops up, butter it and serve it with honey or mix honey and peanut butter together for a yummy honey treat on toast. (If you have children less than one year of age, do not give them honey because of the risk of bacteria. After one year of age, it is not a problem.)

Bee Sweet: Serve a Sunflower

Place a round pineapple slice on a small plate and arrange mandarin orange segments around it in a pinwheel fashion to make the petals. Fill the center of the pineapple ring with dark raisins. Ask, "Do you know what kind of flower this looks like? Would you like to eat some sunflower petals?"

Bee Juice

Serve bubbly cold bee juice by mixing club soda or sparkling water with apple juice. Serve in flowered or fruit-stenciled cups.

Bee Tea

Enjoy hot herb tea with a spoonful of . . . honey!

Story Time

Pick one, two, or all of these great books.

Honey in a Hive by Anne Rockwell—A read-and-find-out-about book about the life and work of honeybees.

The Reason for a Flower by Ruth Heller—A colorful book explaining the importance of birds and bees.

The Bee Tree by Patricia Polacco—A grandpa and his granddaughter are joined by many friends and animals as they chase a bee to his tree, gather honeycomb, and celebrate with a honey and biscuit party. The granddaughter learns that a book is a treasure to be chased, too.

Express Yourself Time

Use these questions to prompt children to express themselves.

- What are some other words that start with the letter *B*?

- Without bees, we would have no fruit. What is your favorite fruit?

- Bees live in hives, which are like our homes, and the bees work to keep the hive going. What do you do at home to help your mom and dad?

Learning Time

The honeybee is one of man's oldest friends. The bee gives us good tasting honey and beeswax, and it also helps grow new plants. Have you ever seen a bee buzz around flowers?

Every hive, or bee home, has one queen bee. She is the ruler of the hive and all the other bees work to build and repair the hive and search for fruit for the bees.

Honeybees do not hibernate, or sleep, during cold weather. They stay alive by eating their stored honey and sharing their body heat. How do we stay warm in the winter time?

Craft and Game Time

Fruit Fun Artwork

Have a bowl of fruit out for children to see as a model for their work. Have them draw, then color or paint their work. They can either draw the whole bowl or just one fruit. Little packs of watercolors work great for those who choose to paint. Always put names and dates on pictures.

Bee Your Best

Have children use yellow construction paper and draw themselves doing a good deed for someone else. You may have to suggest things like helping mom with the dishes or cleaning their room.

Bee Bee Bumblebee Game

Play I Spy with a little twist: "Bee Bee Bumblebee, I see something you don't see and it is (say the color of an object you spy)." The person choosing the object allows three guesses to pass before disclosing the object he has chosen. Take turns in your circle.

Lesson Time

Pleasant words are a honeycomb, sweet to the soul and healing to the bones.
—*Proverbs 16:24*

Application

We know that a honeycomb is sweet. We've already had some honey today that tastes good. The Bible says in this verse that words can also be sweet and "taste" good to our hearts. Don't you like it when your teacher or your mom and dad say good things to you?

Play this sweet word activity to reinforce the lesson.

Have some yellow strips of paper cut ahead of time with these phrases on them:

- Thank you.

- Can I help?

- I like you.

- You are a good friend.

- You have a bright smile.

- You're a happy person.

- You are so sweet.

- You always make my day sunny.

"I have a honey jar full of sweet words. Each one of you will draw one out and we'll read them out loud." (Nonreaders will need a little help.)

Take turns reading the good words.

"How do you feel when someone says kind words to you? We've just collected some sweet honey for our hearts, haven't we? Remember how good it 'tastes' to speak kind words and also to listen to words from others that are 'sweet.' Let's all remember to say good things this week at school and at home."

Prayer Time

Thank you, Lord, for sending bees to help make fruit and flowers. You made so many wonderful things for us to enjoy. Thank you for this tea party with my friends and the kind words we all tasted today. Amen.

Bee Bee Bumble Bee

Jesus lives inside of me

He gives me smiles and words to say

And helps me each and every day.

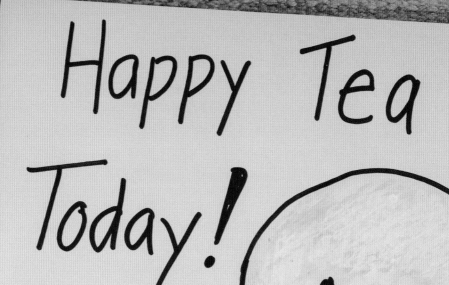

Happy Tea Today!

**Please join me for
a Happy Day Tea Party!**
Wear anything that
makes you happy.

Time:

Place:

Smile

Happy Day Tea

Setting the Scene

- Spread out a quilt, colorful blanket, or piece of fabric on the floor or table. The idea is to use bright and fun fabric.

- After you sit down, ask each child to point to their favorite color or their "happy" color.

- If you have time and can find them, use napkins printed with a smiley face and any cups and small dishes that look festive. Displaying colorful straws adds to the fun.

- Party blowers always make kids smile.

- Make a smiley face out of yellow poster board and a black marker. Have it somewhere in the room or at the door to greet guests.

- Have the children decorate a paper or plastic cup with a smiley face, using a marker.

- Start the party with the song "If You're Happy and You Know It." Everyone can follow along, marching around the quilt as they sing the verses including "If you're happy and you know it, "clap your hands," "stomp your feet," "touch the ground," "turn around," and finally "sit down." (To see this song in its entirety, see page 74.)

Welcome

Greet each child with a hug as they enter and say, "I'm so glad you're here. The day already seems brighter with your nice smile." When the party starts, compliment each child for making an artistic or good choice. Say something like, "I really like the flower on your shirt. Is that one of your favorite colors? I'm glad you wore that to the Happy Day Tea today. You are such a special girl (boy)."

Happy Menu

Happy Face Fruit Plate (This can be done ahead of time or the kids can help you make it.)

- Build a happy face on a brightly colored plate.

- Slice a whole banana from top to bottom and lay it near the edge of the plate as the mouth.

- Make eyes out of dried apricots or round slices of kiwi.

- Top with a purple grape for eyeballs.

- Turn a sliced strawberry upside down for a nose.

- Be creative with the hair. Use grapes, pineapple chunks, or mandarin oranges . . . or try chocolate chips or licorice for brown, black, or red hair.

These are fun to make and yummy to eat!

Funny Face Pizzas

Spread red sauce and a layer of mozzarella cheese on a round English muffin half. Make eyes using sliced green or black olives. You can add eyebrows by adding a sliver of the black olive. After broiling, make a mouth using a slice of red pepper. Give each pizza some hair with either bits of parsley or grated cheddar cheese or both. Encourage the kids to be creative.

Lemon Tea

Just make herbal tea and flavor it with sugar and lemon.

Sunny Lemonade

There's nothing like lemonade to make you smile! Just use pre-mixed lemonade but add fresh lemon slices for the guests to sample. Talk about how sour things need to have sugar added to make them sweeter.

Express Yourself Time

Tell children that the tastes of sweet and sour are both important to our food choices, but our words can also be sweet or sour. Help them understand that sweet words make people happy and sour words make them sad. Ask: "What are some sweet words that could help others feel happy?" (*I like you; you're nice; I like your smile; have a happy day*)

If You're Feeling Really Silly, Play the "Let Me See You Smile" Game

Have children sit in a circle. The object is not to smile or laugh. Have one child look at his neighbor and say, "If you're feeling really silly, let me see you smile." The neighbor child replies, "I'm feeling really silly, but I just can't smile." See how far you can go around the circle until someone laughs or cracks a big smile.

Knock-Knock

Jokes are meant to make people smile. Let the children share a joke with the group. Here are a few to get you started:

Knock, knock. Who's there? Police. Police who? Police sit down so we can start the game.

Knock, knock. Who's there? Radio. Radio who? Radio not, here I come.

Knock, knock. Who's there? Howl. Howl who? Howl it be if I tell you some more jokes?

Knock, knock. Who's there? Honeydew. Honeydew who? Honeydew you love me?

More Jokes. See If You Can Guess:

What do cheerleaders have for breakfast? *Cheer-ios*

What do frogs wear on their feet in summer? *Open toad shoes*

What kind of keys don't open doors? *Piano keys*

What would you get if you crossed a rabbit and a frog? *A bunny ribbit*

What's a mouse's favorite dessert? *Cheesecake*

Story Time

Pick one, two, or all of these fun books.

Ira Sleeps Over by Bernard Waber—A boy who is embarrassed to tell anyone he's afraid to sleep without his teddy bear ends up finding a friend with the same feelings.

I Love You, Stinky Face by Lisa McCourt—A winsome story about a mom who tells her son she will love him no matter what condition he is in.

Amelia Bedelia by Peggy Parish—Silly Amelia misunderstands words and takes everything literally and gets into all kinds of funny situations. There are many books in this series. All will make you smile.

Where the Sidewalk Ends by Shel Silverstein—These fanciful stories and poems address childhood concerns.

Craft Time

Make Someone Smile Card

Think of someone you want to make happy and create a smiley face card to cheer them up. Some ideas for the card message could be: *I'm thinking of you today. Be Happy. God loves you. When I think of you, it makes me happy. Having a friend like you makes me smile.*

Bible verses for your card:

The joy of the Lord is your strength.
—*Nehemiah 8:10*

A happy heart makes the face cheerful.
—*Proverbs 15:13*

Kind words are like honey,
enjoyable and healthful.
—*Proverbs 16:24 (TLB)*

Lesson Time

Is any one of you in trouble? He should pray. Is anyone happy? Let him sing songs of praise.
—James 5:13

Application

Jesus had many feelings. He felt sad when his friend Lazarus died. He felt angry when people were greedy in the temple. He felt happy when people believed He could heal them.

Jesus knows how you feel when you are happy or sad and He wants you to know it's okay to be happy or sad. There are things that happen that make us sad. What did the verse we just read say to do when we are sad or troubled? (*Pray*) God wants us to be happy because He loves us and cares for us. What did we do today when we were happy? (*Sang, smiled*)

Pick a few of these and have the children answer them. You probably won't have time to do them all.

- I feel happy when . . .

- I wish I could . . .

- I would like to be . . .

- I have a good time when . . .

- I feel sad when . . .

- I was surprised when . . .

- I get angry sometimes when . . .

- I feel afraid when . . .

- Today I feel . . .

Have a small box or sack filled with small pieces of paper with these words (emotions) written on them: happy, sad, afraid, silly, worried, angry, surprised.

Tell the children that sometimes we let our emotions show on our faces. Have them each draw out a slip of paper and show the emotion on their face. Let the other children guess which emotion it is. Be sure to end with smiles of happiness!

Prayer Time

Lord, I'm glad you made smiles. It is fun to laugh and play and make other people smile. Thank you for this happy tea with my friends. Amen.

"Smiles"

There are so many happy things
God made in every place;
But the one that I like most of all
Is the smile upon your face.

Please join me for a Home Sweet Home Tea Party!

Wear your red slippers or your hair in braids.

Time:

Place:

Home Sweet Home Tea

Setting the Scene

- Use a large yellow towel or blanket to make a quick "yellow brick road."

- Place a basket on the table to represent the basket in which Dorothy carried her faithful dog. A stuffed puppy would add to the fun.

- Place a simple homemade sign over the table that reads HOME SWEET HOME.

Welcome

Greet your guests with a hug and say, "I'm so glad you're here today. You are special to me. I am happy you're in my home!" Invite each guest to "follow the yellow brick road" to a fun tea about home.

Story Time

Pick one or both of these great books.

The Wizard of Oz by L. Frank Baum—Young Dorothy dreams she has a journey in another land. Even though she meets many wonderful friends, she realizes that there is "no place like home." There are many editions of this classic tale. Find one that's short enough to read and enjoy at a tea party. After you read the story, ask: "What did Dorothy and each of her friends hope the Wizard would give them?"

The Three Little Pigs by Paul Galdone—Any version of this classic tale will do. Three little pigs build three different houses. They realize that one is the safest and best. Ask: "What did each pig use to make his house? Which took the longest to make? Which house was the best? Why?"

Home Sweet Home Menu

Three Little Pigs Houses

After you've read or told the story of *The Three Little Pigs*, create edible houses for each pig. Guests can choose one house to create or make all three. They will have fun building and nibbling.

Stick House

Pretzels are the perfect edible sticks and peanut butter is the perfect mortar. Give each child a paper plate and some pretzels and let the fun begin. A little dab of peanut butter is all they need. Be sure that none of your little guests is allergic to peanuts.

Straw House

Whole wheat crackers or shredded wheat biscuits make great "straw" and, once again, use peanut butter to hold it together.

Brick House

Graham crackers divided on the lines make delicious "bricks." Be sure to add a cracker chimney to your house and use peanut butter to hold it together.

Sweet Little Pigs

Create a plump little pig body by using one large and one mini marshmallow stuck together with half a toothpick. Add pretzel sticks for the legs and a piece of curly dry pasta for the tail.

Cheesy Yellow Brick Road

After reading or talking about *The Wizard of Oz*, your guests can make an edible yellow brick road with square cheese crackers. Add two red candies (M&M's will work) for the ruby slippers. Have them "walk" their red M&M's down the yellow brick road as they repeat "There's no place like home." Let them eat their M&M's when they get to the end of the road.

Heavenly Home Vanilla Milk Tea

Serve milk in teacups with a half teaspoon of vanilla extract added for flavor. Top with mini marshmallows. As they sip, you can talk about God's heavenly home beyond the clouds. Another option is hot chocolate topped with mini marshmallows.

Craft Time

You may not have time for all of these projects, so just choose one and have fun.

My House

Have children draw a picture of their own house and then color it with crayons, colored pencils, or markers. Encourage them also to draw family members and pets.

Make a House

Cut two house shapes per child out of construction paper. (Use the "Home Sweet Home" template in the back of the book.) One will be the inside of the house, one the outside. (For an easier version, use the "Simple House" template in the back of the book, which requires no gluing or cutting.)

- On the outside house pattern, cut three sides of each window and the door, leaving the fold line attached to make flaps that open.

- Use a glue stick to spread glue on the back of the house. Do not put glue on the windows and door.

- Press the two house shapes together. Now you can peek inside each opening.

- Each child can use crayons and markers to draw inside the openings the people and pets who live in their house or apartment.

Sharing Time

Ask each child to share their construction-paper house with the group and answer these questions, "Who lives in your home? What is your favorite room in your house?"

If you need more things to talk about, ask the guests to name any other places where they have lived or if they can think of different kinds of homes people live in. (Examples: house, apartment, condominium, tent, tepee, hut, igloo.)

Learning Time

God has provided special homes for all of his creatures. Let's talk about those special homes.

Where does a rabbit live? (*Burrow*)

Where does a bird live? (*Nest*)

What animals live on a farm? (*Cows, pigs, horses, sheep, chickens, ducks*)

Name some animals you think live in the forest? (*Bears, hawks, eagles, snakes, owls, porcupines, hedgehogs*)

Which animals live in the rainforest? (*Chimpanzees, gorillas, pygmy hippopotamuses, iguanas, platypuses, tigers*)

Which animals would be able to live in freezing Antarctica? (*Polar bears, penguins*)

Do you know of any animals or creatures that live underground? (*Gophers, ground squirrels, moles, rabbits, skunks, worms, ants*)

Who lives in a hive? (*Bees*)

Do you know what animals or creatures you'd find living in the desert? (*Ants, antelope, camels, armadillos, bats, skinks, spiders, boa constrictors, bobcats, bighorn sheep, coyotes*)

You might want to check out more information about animals and their habitats on the Internet and print out pictures of some of these animals.

Lesson Time

Do not let your hearts be troubled. Trust in God; trust also in me.
In my Father's house are many rooms; if it were not so, I would have told you.
I am going there to prepare a place for you.
—*John 14: 1–2*

Application

Jesus tells his friends about a wonderful home God is getting ready for all of us in heaven. It's a mansion with many rooms—and there's a room for you and me if we trust in our Heavenly Father. Jesus tells his friends the way to find the house He's preparing. He says, "I am the way." If we have Jesus living in our hearts, He will take us

there someday. A home in heaven is waiting for us that is more beautiful than we could imagine.

What do you think heaven will be like? Do you know anyone who already lives there? If we love Jesus, we will be able to live with Him in that heavenly place one day, too.

Prayer Time

God in heaven, thank you for the home I live in and for each person who lives there with me. Thank you for this fun tea party today. Someday I want to see the beautiful house you have made for me in heaven. Amen.

*H*ome is where
I live and grow,
*I*t's always where
I want to go.

**Be an angel and join me
for an Angel Tea Party!**
Wear anything white or fluffy
or just wear a beautiful smile.
Halos optional!

Time:
Place:

Angel Tea

Angel Tea Party

Setting the Scene

- Each child's name can be printed on paper angel place cards—see directions for making these later in the Craft Time section.

- Set teacups on white doilies. Use white doilies for an angelic look all over the room.

- Have pictures of angels found in magazines, books, or old Christmas cards placed on the table.

- Any figurines you might have of angels can be placed around the room.

- Light votive candles for a heavenly atmosphere.

Welcome

Greet each child as they enter and say, "It's going to be a heavenly day today! Have you ever heard someone say 'You're an angel?' Well, today at our tea party we are going to learn more about angels and what they are really like."

Heavenly Menu

Angels on Cloud Nine

With the simple, just-add-water angel food cake mixes today, this is a quick and easy dessert to make, or go to your local grocery store and buy one. Cut the cake into angel shapes by pressing a cookie cutter into thick slices. Make angel food stars with a star-shaped cookie cutter. Place dollops of frozen whipped topping or whipped cream on a plate and let the angels and stars "float" in the clouds.

Heavenly Punch

Place large spoonfuls of lemon (white) sherbet in a punch bowl. Add equal amounts of lemon-lime soda and ginger ale for a fun, foamy, heavenly treat.

Craft Time

Angel Place Cards

- With sturdy white paper, draw an angel shape (see template in back of book).

  - Fold and tape the tab on the bottom to make the angel stand up.

  - Write each child's name on a place card.

Tiny Angels

Purchase a bag of peanuts in the shell. Give each child a large peanut. Have them draw a

face and halo on the top with a marker. Cut a hole in a small doily or a round piece of fabric and slip the pretty "dress" over the peanut angel.

This can also be done with a wooden clothespin for the body. Draw dots on the top for eyes and use bits of thread, curly ribbon, or packing straw glued on top for hair. Paper wings can be added to the back with glue for more fun.

Angel Drawings

Look at beautiful angel pictures in art books or a collection of old Christmas and gift cards. Draw your own angel or trace an angel shape from a cookie cutter, then color and design your own angel.

Story and Picture Time

Pick one or two of these great renderings of angels by famous artists to look at.

Akiane: Her Life, Her Art, Her Poetry by Akiane Kramarik—This book is a true account of a young Lithuanian girl who started painting when she was four years old. Her angel pictures are full of light and her story will amaze you and the children. God speaks to children and helps them see His love on earth.

"The Annunciation" by Fra Angelico—This classic painting can be used to show children different interpretations of angels from long ago.

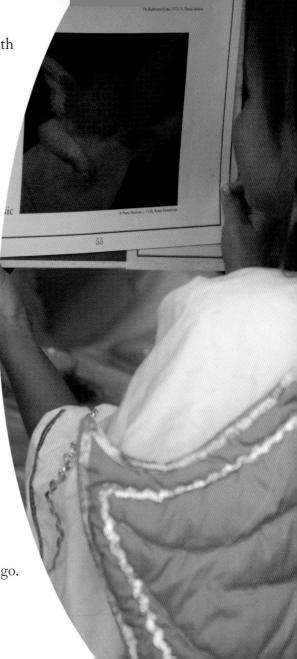

The ABCs of Art (Baby Einstein) by Julie Aigner-Clark

"Angel Annunciating" by Lorenzo Lotto will give children another famous angel image.

Express Yourself Time

For many years great artists have enjoyed painting angels. The artists would read the Bible, pray, and then paint what they imagined about angels from the stories they read. The best place for us to find out what angels are like and what they do is in the Bible. We don't really know what angels look like but we know they are always praising God. What do you think angels look like?

Great artists who painted angels usually separated them from humans in the picture with a wall or a curtain or an instrument. In these pictures, do you see a wall or a column or a flower that makes a separation between the angel and humans? (Show them the pictures you found in the art book.) The artist was telling us that humans and angels are not the same. However, there are lots of stories in the Bible where angels appeared on earth and talked to humans. They looked just like ordinary people. God sent them as messengers to help people.

How do you think angels work today? Let's read a story about God's angels from the Bible.

Lesson Time

Jacob left Beersheba and set out for Haran. When he reached a certain place, he stopped for the night because the sun had set. Taking one of the stones there, he put it under his head and lay down to sleep. He had a dream in which he saw a stairway resting on the earth, with its top reaching to heaven, and the angels of God were ascending and descending on it. There above it stood the Lord, and he said: "I am the Lord, the God of your father Abraham and the God of Isaac. I will give you and your descendants the land on which you are lying. Your descendants will be like the dust of the earth, and you will spread out to the west and to the east, to the north and to the south. All peoples on earth will be blessed through you and your offspring. I am with you and will watch over you wherever you go,

and I will bring you back to this land. I will not leave you until I have done what I have promised you." When Jacob awoke from his sleep, he thought, "Surely the Lord is in this place, and I was not aware of it." He was afraid and said, "How awesome is this place! This is none other than the house of God; this is the gate of heaven." —Genesis 28:10–17

Application

God is good and will be with you always. Angels are helpers for God. In the Bible we read about angels who told people what to do and where to go. Sometimes angels visited people while they were dreaming, like we just read in this story. Have you ever had a dream? Do you remember your dreams when you wake up the next morning?

Do you remember what Jacob used for a pillow? That's right, a rock. Ouch! That probably wasn't very comfortable. What do you sleep with at night when you go to bed? Do you snuggle with a blanket? Or a teddy bear or special toy?

Jacob dreamed about a huge ladder that looked like a stairway reaching all the way to heaven from his bed. What was climbing up and down that ladder? Angels! Yes, lots of God's angels. Then in Jacob's dream he heard God speak. He told Jacob that his family would make people on earth happy and blessed.

Most angels who visited people in the Bible said things like, "Be of good cheer," or "Don't be afraid," or "God has heard your prayer."

Maybe your mom sometimes calls you an angel. Do you know how to make people happy? Making people happy is a great job for an angel.

What are some ways you could make someone happy today? (*Smile, sing a song, tell someone not to be afraid, draw a picture for someone, tell someone that God loves them*) How

can you praise God like the angels do? (*Say thank you to Him, sing a song, pray*)

Singing Time

Children love to sing. If you are not a singer, don't fret, let the children sing to you. Tell them that the songs we sing at church are designed to praise God. The Bible tells us in Revelation (4:8) that angels sing day and night. Cherubim and seraphim, referred to in the following song, are different kinds of angels with many wings.

If you know this song, you can teach it to them or sing it to them. If you do not, ask them if they know any songs that praise God, such as "Praise Him, All Ye Little Children," and sing it together.

"Holy, Holy, Holy"

Holy, holy, holy! Lord God Almighty!

Early in the morning our song shall rise to Thee; (*wiggle fingers from your mouth to the sky*)

Holy, holy, holy, merciful and mighty! *(open hands in kindness, then make a strong fist)*

God, in three Persons, blessed Trinity! (*hold three fingers up, then point to heaven with one*)

Holy, holy, holy! Lord God Almighty! All the saints adore Thee, (*circle your hands as you raise them higher*)

Casting down their golden crowns around the glassy sea; (*pretend you are taking off your crown and lay it down in front of you on the ground*)

Cherubim and seraphim, falling down before Thee, (*spread out arms like flapping wings and bow down*)

Who was, and is, and evermore shall be (*look up toward heaven*).

Prayer Time

God, you love us so much that You send us helpers. You are always with us. Thank you for good friends and for all the fun at this Angel Tea Party. Amen.

*T*he angel of the Lord
encamps around those
who fear Him.
—*Psalm 34:7*

*H*e shall give His angels
charge over you to keep
you in all your ways.
—*Psalm 91:11*

*P*raise the Lord, you His
angels, you mighty ones who
do His bidding, who obey His
Word. Praise the Lord, all His
heavenly hosts, you His
servants who do His will.
—*Psalm 103:20-21*

Hands and Feet Tea

Setting the Scene

- Colorful teacups and bright plates will make the room cheery.

- Display pictures cut from magazines of hands and feet doing fun activities around the room. Just mount them on colorful construction paper.

- Have a workstation set up with paper, tracing pencils, markers, and scissors for older children.

Welcome

Greet each guest with a high five and say, "Welcome to our tea party. I'm so glad you're here. We're going to have such fun with our hands and feet today." Invite children to select a pencil or marker to trace their hands and feet.

Hands and Feet Menu

You don't have to use all of these ideas, but there are plenty here for you to choose from. Kids love them all!

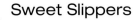

Sweet Slippers

Using a peanut-shaped cookie, make a foot slipper that is sweet enough to eat. Dip one end of the cookie in Cool Whip and sprinkle some coconut (optional) over it. This can be done ahead of time and served to the children or they can help make them.

Peanut Butter and Jelly Mittens

Make a peanut butter and jelly sandwich, and then place a mitten shape on top. If you can find a mitten cookie cutter, all the better. Cut the shape out and serve some real "finger food" on each child's tea plate.

Yummy Fingertips

Trace each child's hand on a piece of paper. For a special touch, use colored candies on the traced fingertips for nail polish. This will be every young guest's favorite "manicure." The only good reason to bite a fingernail!

Fizzy Sweet Tea

Add an equal amount of orange juice to sparkling water or ginger ale and sip away. You can substitute cold herb tea for the soda if you don't want the fizz. Give each child a spoon and let them stir the drink.

Story Time

Pick one, two, or all of these great books.

The Kissing Hand by Audrey Penn—A mother raccoon sends her anxious child to his first day of school with a special reminder of her constant love on his hand.

Hand, Hand, Fingers, Thumb by Al Perkins—A lively rhyming book to delight children.

The Foot Book by Dr. Seuss—A fun book of rhymes to twist your tongue and give your imagination a tickle.

The Mitten by Jan Brett—A child's lost mitten becomes quite an animal habitat.

Express Yourself Time

This is a great time to sing a few of the following songs.

"The Eensy-Weensy Spider" (use fingers to act out the words)
The eensy weensy spider
Crawled up the water spout
Down came the rain
And washed the spider out
Out came the sun
And dried up all the rain
And the eensy weensy spider
Crawled up the spout again.

"If You're Happy and You Know It"

If you're happy and you know it, clap your hands (*clap clap*)
If you're happy and you know it, clap your hands (*clap clap*)
If you're happy and you know it, then your face will surely show it
If you're happy and you know it, clap your hands (*clap clap*)

If you're happy and you know it, stomp your feet (*stomp stomp*)
If you're happy and you know it, stomp your feet (*stomp stomp*)

If you're happy and you know it, then your face will surely show it
If you're happy and you know it, stomp your feet (*stomp stomp*)

If you're happy and you know it, shout "Hurray!" (*hoo-ray!*)
If you're happy and you know it, shout "Hurray!" (*hoo-ray!*)
If you're happy and you know it, then your face will surely show it
If you're happy and you know it, shout "Hurray!" (*hoo-ray!*)

If you're happy and you know it, do all three (*clap clap, stomp stomp, hoo-ray!*)
If you're happy and you know it, do all three (*clap clap, stomp stomp, hoo-ray!*)
If you're happy and you know it, then your face will surely show it
If you're happy and you know it, do all three (*clap clap, stomp stomp, hoo-ray!*)

Our hands and feet are especially important when we use them to help others. How can you help others with your hands and feet?

Have children use the following activity to reinforce helping hands.

Sit in a circle facing someone's back and use your hands to give a shoulder massage to the person in front of you. Then turn around and give a shoulder rub to the person on the other side.

Craft Time

Flower Power Place Card

- Make a flower by tracing a hand with open fingers or use the template in the back of the book.

- Trace two feet onto sturdy paper and color them green for leaves, or trace feet on green construction paper. Then cut out the "leaves."

- Make the stem out of sturdy paper wide enough to fit the child's name and long enough to fold in half and stand up on the table (about one and a half inches wide and eight inches long).

- Write the child's name on the stem and add this verse: Walk as children of light. (Ephesians 5:8)

Butterfly Feet

- Trace the child's feet with their feet crossed at the ankles or use the template in the back of this book (big toe toward outside of the paper). These footprints will be the butterfly wings.

- Draw a black body down the center for the butterfly and add two long antennae at the top.

- Color and decorate the wings with beautiful colors. Be sure to write the child's name on the back of their butterfly and date it.

The Gift of a Hug

- Use a grocery sack or any large piece of paper.

- Have the child lay down on the paper with their arms stretched out while you trace around their hands and arms to make one long arm span.

- Cut along the traced line and have the child write their name and the date with the words "A Hug from _____" inside.

- Roll it into a spool and have them save it to give to someone who needs a hug. (Grandparents love this gift.)

Game Time

Guessing Hands

Before the game, select a few small objects for guessing and put them aside in a secret place. (A marble, Lego building block, golf ball, jack, toy car, paper clip, crayon, or button are good choices.) Put one object into the guessing sock without the guests seeing it. Let one child feel the outside of the sock and guess what's inside. If he cannot figure it out, allow him to reach inside the sock (without looking) and touch the object. After an object has been correctly named, let the next child feel something different. Just once around and everyone will notice how our hands are tools that help us explore by touching.

Lesson Time

Whatever your hand finds to do, do it with all your might.
—*Ecclesiastes 9:10 (NASB)*

Application

Marked by the Master: You're a Miracle

Look at your palm while cupping your hand. Do you see the lines in your palm that look like the letter *M*? Did you know that God made your hands? That *M* can remind you of three important things.

1. God *m*ade you and

2. God *m*arked you to remind you that . . .

3. You are a *m*iracle.

You are marked by the master and He has a wonderful future planned for your whole life! Now that's something to clap about, to get excited about.

Find the *M*-shaped line on your palm and say, "I'm a miracle!"

Look at each other's hands and see if you can find the *M*. Say to your friend, "You're a miracle!" Yes, every one of you is a miracle.

Now, let's not forget about our feet.

> How beautiful upon the mountains are the feet of those
> who bring good news of peace and salvation.
> —*Isaiah 52:7*

Our feet take us to places we want to go, don't they? Do you know why we made a butterfly with our footprints? Butterflies are beautiful and they fly from flower to flower. God says our feet can be beautiful when we bring good news to others. The story of Jesus and His love is good news. Great news! He lives in heaven and thinks about you all the time. He loves you and your friends, too. I feel like running and telling my friends that they are very special and that Jesus loves them and so do I. What friend do you wish you could run to and visit with today? What good news would you bring to them? Maybe you could show them the *M* inside their hand and say, "You're a miracle."

Prayer Time

Thank you, Lord, for giving us hands and feet. Help me to do kind things with my hands. I want my feet to take me where You want me to go. Help me remember that I am a miracle! Amen.

Clap your hands and tap your feet

Having tea is oh, so sweet.

Come, everyone, and clap your hands for joy!
—*Psalm* 47:1 NLT

Please join me for a
Teddy Bear Picnic Tea!
Bring your favorite teddy bear
and join the fun.

Time:
Place:

Teddy Bear Picnic Tea

Setting the Scene

- Spread a fun quilt or blanket either outside or inside, depending on the weather.

- Place a teddy bear–face place card with each child's name on it around the quilt. (See template in back of book.) Children can make a place card for their bears once they arrive. Have cut-out patterns ready for coloring ahead of time.

- Have paper plates and crayons set out for each guest. Many grocery stores have paper plates with bears on them. If you can't find them, any plates will do.

- Prepare a brown-paper, teddy bear lunch sack for each guest. Using a black marker, draw a bear face on the bag and cut out just above the ear line.

- Have a small bowl of Teddy Grahams shaped like little bears in a bowl for appetizers.

Welcome

Give hello hugs to each guest and say, "I'm so glad you brought your teddy along for a picnic tea party today!" Be sure to welcome each bear.

Bear Menu

To be served any time your tummies *growl* at the tea party.

Teddy Bear Peanut Butter and Jelly Sandwiches (either prepared beforehand or with the children's help)

These are fun to make and kids love them. Children can press a bear cookie cutter into two slices of brown bread (one slice at a time) and help to spread jam or honey and peanut butter onto the bear-shaped pieces. If you don't have a bear cookie cutter, try cutting a teddy out of the bread with a kitchen knife. Wrap up the bear sandwich and put it in the brown paper bear bag with a napkin for the picnic.

Panda Bear Ice Cream Cup

Place one round scoop of vanilla ice cream in a small bowl, add black chocolate cookie ears, chocolate-chip eyes, and a licorice or cut Tootsie Roll for the mouth. He's almost too cute to eat! The scoop can be made ahead of time, and frozen, and the kids only add ears and eyes.

Bear Snacks

Have any type of chips, mini carrots, or raisins available for children to put in a small bag and add to their lunch or have baggies ready ahead of time.

Bear-y Sweet Tea

Serve cold herb tea and let children

sweeten it with honey. Tell them that bears love honey.

Panda Bear Punch

White milk with a drizzle of chocolate syrup on top makes a delicious drink.

Story Time

There are plenty of bear stories to choose from. Here are some that I like:

We're Going on a Bear Hunt by Michael Rosen—This delightful picture book about a father and his children who hunt for a bear is a fun book to act out. Later in this chapter, you will find instructions for the motions.

Little Bear books by Else Holmelund Minarik—This is a loveable series of books about animal friends and their adventures with each other.

Corduroy by Don Freeman—The endearing story of a forgotten bear and the little girl who wants him.

Express Yourself Time

Have the children take turns introducing their teddy to everyone. Encourage each person to hold the guest bear in front of them so everyone can see.

Tell the children that sometimes we think of our favorite teddy bear as a good friend because it sits with us and makes us smile or gives us a hug. Ask what they can do to make others smile and feel loved. (*Smile, listen to them, hug them, sit or read with them quietly*)

The younger children will enjoy a game called Walking 'Round the Garden with My Teddy Bear. Walk your fingers around their outstretched palm and up their arm repeating, "Walking 'round the garden with my teddy bear, one step, two steps, tickle under there," as you tickle softly under their chin.

For older guests, try the body motions to *We're Going on a Bear Hunt.* Have children stand in a circle and repeat after the leader, mimicking all the actions of the leader. You will do this same verse several times, changing whatever you are pretending to see with each verse.

Leader: We're going on a bear hunt! (*Everyone marches in place and repeats*)
Oh, look! I see some grass. (*Hands over eyes looking and children repeat*)
Can't go around it. (*Hands stretch wide and children repeat*)
Can't go under it. (*Hands reach low and children repeat*)
Can't go over it. (*Hands reach high and children repeat*)
Gotta go through it. (*Start marching again*)

Repeat using these different scenarios:

Lake (last verse: *Gotta swim across it—make swimming motion with arms*)

Tall tree (last verse: *Gotta climb it—make climbing motion with arms*)

Last time through:

Oh, look! I see a cave! Let's go down and see what is inside!

Oooo . . . it's cold in here!

I feel something warm . . .

I feel something furry . . .
It's a bear! (*Run in place and then repeat motions in reverse order very quickly, saying:*)
Up the tree (*climbing motion*)
Across the lake (*swimming motion*)
Through the grass (*waving grass motion*)
We're safe! (*Whew!*)

Learning Time

If time allows, choose some bear pictures from magazines or print from the Internet some pictures of real bears in their natural habitat.

There are many different kinds of bears. Can you name some different kinds? (*Brown, grizzly, panda, polar, black, koala, teddy*)

Baby bears are called *cubs* and bears love to eat things like fish, berries, leaves, and picnic lunches from campers.

How do you think real bears sleep? (*In the fall, bears get ready for the long winter by eating and eating as much food as they can find on trees and in streams. When they are really fat, the cold weather comes and the berries and fish are gone. Bears hibernate in a hollow tree or cave. All winter long they don't eat anything at all but they sleep and only move around to change positions. In the springtime, they come out of their dens very skinny and hungry. What do you think they want to do? They eat and eat and eat all spring, summer, and fall until it's time again for another long winter's nap.*)

Lesson Time

Love bears all things, hopes all things, endures all things.
—*1 Corinthians 13:7 (ESV)*

No matter how much we love our teddy bears, God loves us even more. He loves us so much He sent His Son to die for us. Because of His love for us, we need to love others and be kind and patient with them. Especially people in our own homes, like our brothers and sisters!

Craft Time

You may not have time to do all of these, just pick your favorite.

Bear Pictures

Children can draw and color a picture of their bear on a

sturdy paper plate and use it at picnic time. Templates for bears are in the back of the book.

Teddy Bear Paper Dolls

Using the template in the back of the book, you can make copies before the party and have children color their own teddy bear doll. Children can add a paper apron and attach ribbons on the shoulders to dress their paper doll bear.

Bear-y Special Bookmark

Use the template in the back of the book to make copies of the bookmark or have children make their own. They will write *Love Bears All Things* on the top and add a teddy face or a heart to color. Each guest can give the bookmark as a gift or save it for their own special book.

Prayer Time

Lord, thank you for cuddly bears that make us happy. Help me to be a good friend to someone this week. Thank you for this fun teddy bear party today. Amen.

*Y*ou can tell any secret to your teddy bear and he won't be shocked or tell anyone else.

Please join me for an Asian Tea Party!
Wear a colorful short bathrobe with a sash as a kimono and flowers in your hair or just wear a smile!

Time:

Place:

Asian Tea Today

Asian Tea Party

Setting the Scene

- Look for anything from Asia that you have in your house—vases, silk fabric, etc.

- Dress a doll in silk fabric wrapped like a kimono and use as a centerpiece.

- If you have a world globe, place it where the guests can spin it to see Asia and find the countries of Japan, China, Vietnam, Korea, and Thailand.

- Have guests sit on the floor, which is the Japanese custom. Put rugs or small bath towels on the floor for them to sit on.

- Paper flowers or fans can be arranged in a cup or vase for a centerpiece, too.

- If you have time, visit a local Asian restaurant and purchase chopsticks, fortune cookies, and place mats. Some paper goods stores have great selections of Asian decorations such as paper umbrellas, chopsticks, and teacups.

- Cups with no handles are traditionally Asian. They may be hard to find but make a great addition to the atmosphere.

- Have guests remove their shoes when they arrive.

Welcome

Greet each guest with a smile and bow at the waist to say "welcome." You may also say good afternoon in Japanese, *konichiwa*. Everyone takes off their shoes at the door but may wear their socks if they wish.

Asian Menu

Rice Cake Delight

Purchase small rice cakes and serve them with peanut butter, jam, or honey for a fast and easy treat.

Sweet Sushi

Cut a large marshmallow in half and press the sticky side into rice cereal. Roll a flat piece of Fruit by the Foot, found in the fruit snack and cereal aisle at the grocery store, around the cut marshmallow. Place your colorful and yummy sweet "sushi" on a plate covered with rice cereal. This treat is fun to eat with chop sticks.

Tea from the East

A tradition in Asia is to drink tea from cups with no handles. The tradition began because people wanted

to warm their hands on cold days and would cradle the cup and hold it close to their faces. If you don't have cups without handles, cradle any teacup in your hands and enjoy green herb tea sweetened with honey.

Express Yourself Time

In China, children collect crickets as pets because they cannot keep a dog or a cat in the house. Crickets sing a pretty song and entertain children. Cricket cages are sold in markets and some are very fancy, but some children make their own cage. The cricket lives in their room and cheers them up every time it sings.

What pets do you have?
What cheers you up?
Do you think you'd like to have a cricket as a pet?
Do you have a favorite song?

Story Time

A Pair of Red Clogs by Masako Matsuno—This is a story about a young Japanese girl who is tempted to do something dishonest in order to get a pair of new clogs she longs for.

96 Tea Parties with a Purpose

Talk about a missionary. Explain to children the importance of missionary work and that one missionary who worked in China was named Hudson Taylor. He founded the China Inland Mission and spent five years translating the New Testament into the Ningpo dialect. By the end of his life, in 1905, there were 205 stations with 849 missionaries, and 125,000 Chinese Christians in the China Inland Mission.

Craft Time

Edible Cricket Cage

- Cut an orange into round slices.

- Lay one slice on a plate and put a grape or raisin inside to be your "singing cricket."

- Stick toothpicks vertically around the edge of the orange slice.

- Press another orange slice on the top of the toothpicks to form the top of the cage.

- Now you have a little cage for your sweet grape "cricket." (You'll have to do the singing yourself!)

Paper Fans

- Give each child a sheet of plain white paper.

- Have them draw and color flowers on the long top half of the paper.

- Fold the paper into one-inch folds back and forth from end to end.

- Press the edges firmly to make the fan lines stay in place.

- Wrap a ribbon or rubber band around the bottom before opening up your creation.

Paper Flowers

- Open a round coffee filter and smooth out the pleats.

- Place it on a round dinner plate and let each guest paint the edge with bright watercolor paint.

- After it dries, pull the center and twist to make a flower.

- Tie with a rubber band or add a pretty ribbon.

- Place your flowers in a dry vase on the table as a centerpiece or carry as a bouquet.

Lesson Time

For as high as the heavens are above the earth, so great is His love for those
who fear Him; as far as the east is from the west,
so far has He removed our transgressions from us.
—Psalm 103:11–12

Application

Many Christian missionaries go to countries like China, Thailand, Vietnam, Korea, and Japan to tell the people there about Jesus. Long ago (in 1854) a man named Hudson Taylor went to China to be a missionary. It was not easy to leave his familiar country and customs, but he gave years of his life to be with the people he loved, the people in China. He prayed for the people in Asia. We can pray for the missionaries and for the new believers in Jesus in these countries, too.

A sweet song from the smallest voice cheers the soul.

Prayer Time

Lord, thank you for making a big world with lots of different people. It was fun to have tea surrounded by beautiful things and customs from countries like China and Japan. Bless the missionaries, the people, and the children of countries in the East. Amen.

Please join me for a
Happy Birthday Jesus Tea Party!
Wear green or red or anything that celebrates Christmas.

Time:
Place:

Happy Birthday Jesus Tea Party

Setting the Scene

Since this party is celebrated at Christmas, the house already should be festive.

- As a focal point, place a nativity scene in the center of the table. It will need to be one that can be touched by little hands.

- A decorated gift box without the top on it can provide a fun way to hold paper and markers ready for craft time.

- Either buy or make a birthday cake with *Happy Birthday Jesus* on the top or put three candles on a cookie, cupcake, or cup filled halfway up with uncooked rice.

- A small basket or gift bag to hold candy canes will come in handy later in the party to hold slips of paper for "word gifts."

Welcome

Greet guests at the door with a warm hug and say, "We're glad you came to celebrate with us!" This is a special time of the year.

Celebration Menu

Cranberry-Ginger Tea

Mix equal parts of cranberry juice, ginger ale, and seltzer water to make a cold Christmas drink. Serve in teacups. Yum.

Peppermint Hot Chocolate

Garnish a cup of steaming hot chocolate with whipped cream from the can (let the kids squirt it on) and garnish with a peppermint stick.

Heavenly Yogurt Smoothies

Add sliced strawberries and a tablespoon of honey to a cup of plain yogurt and swirl in the blender to make a creamy treat. Serve in your favorite heavenly teacups. (An orange variation can be whipped up with a tablespoon of frozen orange juice concentrate, a tablespoon of honey, and a pinch of cinnamon.)

Christmas Cookies

Any cookies, either homemade or store-bought, decorated for the season, are perfect to serve at this tea party.

Craft Time

Peanut Nativity

This miniature craft is easy to make and allows each child to have a nativity scene to take home. You will need to purchase a bag of peanuts in the shell and have some jar lids available.

- Sort through the peanuts to find two whole large peanuts and one smaller round peanut in the shell per child attending.

- Have children draw a face and head covering on the larger peanut shells to represent Mary and Joseph. The head covering can be drawn on or a small piece of fabric can be glued on.

- Put a little circle and two dots for eyes on the smaller Baby Jesus peanut.

- Use a small jar lid for the manger. Pour uncooked white or brown rice deep enough to hold the peanut figures in place to represent hay. If kids spill the rice, let them gather the "hay" back into the manger and play with their little nativity figures.

- Use extra peanuts to make angels, shepherds, or wise men.

Happy Birthday Card for Jesus

Birthday cards are a part of every birthday celebration. Let each child make a card for Jesus. You may want to place some cards on the table for inspiration, but it's not necessary. With colored markers and paper, everyone will have a special picture and message to share.

Express Yourself Time

Christmas Carols

Christmas carols are a big part of celebrating the season. Choose a Christmas carol that is familiar and let all the children join in the singing. Some great songs are "Joy to the World," "Hark! The Herald Angels Sing," or "Angels We Have Heard on High." Each are easy and beautifully present the true story of Christmas. If you're running short on time, have the children sing while they do their card or have music playing in the background.

Word Gifts for Jesus

What do you think Jesus would want as a gift from you and me? The Bible says He wants our hearts to love Him and our actions to obey what He tells us in the Bible. Let's put some word gifts written on slips of paper in the gift bag for Jesus. Write down something you know Jesus would want for Christmas. The fruits of the Spirit are always on Jesus' wish list. Let's look at some of these and say how we can apply the word as a gift in our family and with our friends.

Cut strips of paper and have pens so the guests can write words that will be gifts for the giving presentation.

Story Time

Pick one or both of these great books.

The Legend of the Candy Cane by Lori Walburg—A candy store owner tells how the candy cane represents Jesus. The shape represents a shepherd's staff and the letter *J* for Jesus, the red is for the blood of Jesus, and the white stripe is how Jesus washes us white as snow. Each child will love holding their candy cane as you read the story.

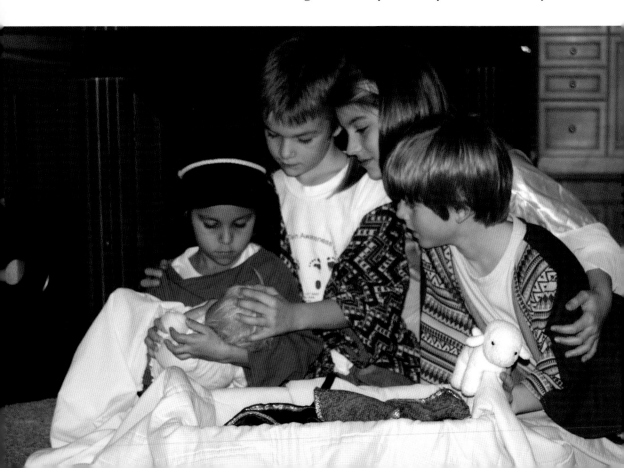

The Christmas Miracle of Jonathan Toomey by Susan Wojciechowski—A grumpy man finds joy again when a widow and her son ask him to carve nativity figures.

Lesson Time

Read these verses to the children to help them think of a word to give back to Jesus.

The fruit of the Spirit is love, joy, peace, patience, kindness, goodness, faithfulness, gentleness, and self-control.
—*Galatians 5:22–23*

Clothe yourselves with compassion, kindness, gentleness, humility, and patience.
—*Colossians 3:12*

Finally, all of you, live in harmony with one another; be sympathetic, love as brothers, be compassionate and humble.
—*1 Peter 3:8*

Application

Before the words are put in the gift bag, have children share the word they chose with the group.

Nativity Play (This activity is optional and would have to be done after the tea party, when parents arrive to pick up their children.)
If time allows, help the children put on a play depicting the birth of Jesus. Use kitchen

*O*h, come let us adore Him, Oh come let us adore Him, *C*hrist the Lord.

towels as shepherd head coverings and white nightgowns or sheets for the angels. The children can help make their costumes from bathrobes and fabric pieces. Using a children's Bible, the angel reads the Christmas story from Luke 2 and the children act out the parts. Get your camera ready and snap away at the scene. This tradition in our family has spanned decades. Both dolls and infant siblings have played the part of Baby Jesus. We treasure the pictures and memories and we pull them out every year. All the parents of your guests will enjoy seeing the interaction and creativity of the children who present the nativity story.

Prayer Time

Jesus, we are glad You were born. We had fun at this birthday party for You today and we hope you like our cards and gifts. Amen.

Templates

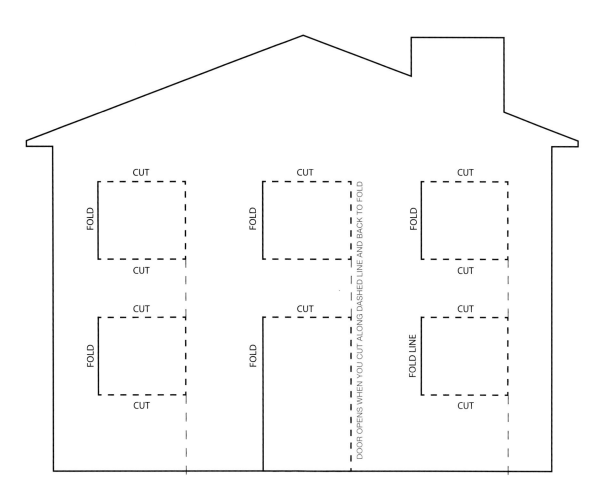

CUT

FOLD

CUT

CUT

FOLD

CUT

CUT

FOLD

CUT

CUT

FOLD

CUT

CUT

FOLD

CUT

CUT

FOLD LINE

CUT

DOOR OPENS WHEN YOU CUT ALONG DASHED LINE AND BACK TO FOLD

Template for Home Sweet Home Tea House —cut two per child—113

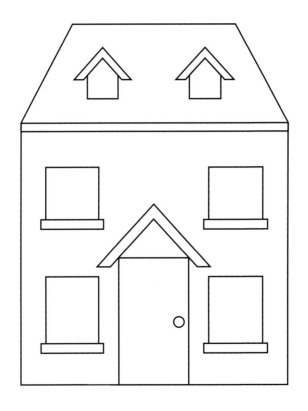

114–Front of Simple House Card

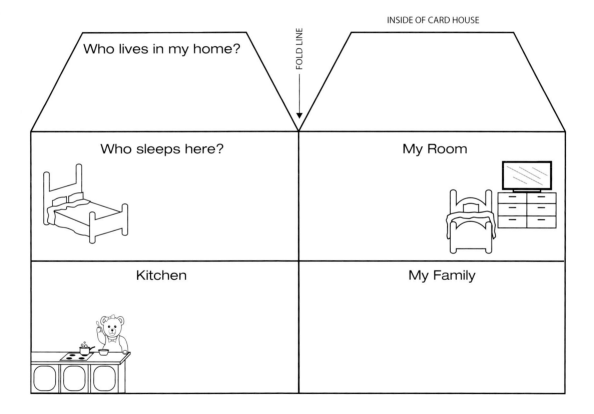

FOLD LINE

INSIDE OF CARD HOUSE

Who lives in my home?

Who sleeps here?

My Room

Kitchen

My Family

Inside of Simple House Card–115

116—Templates for Angel Tea Party

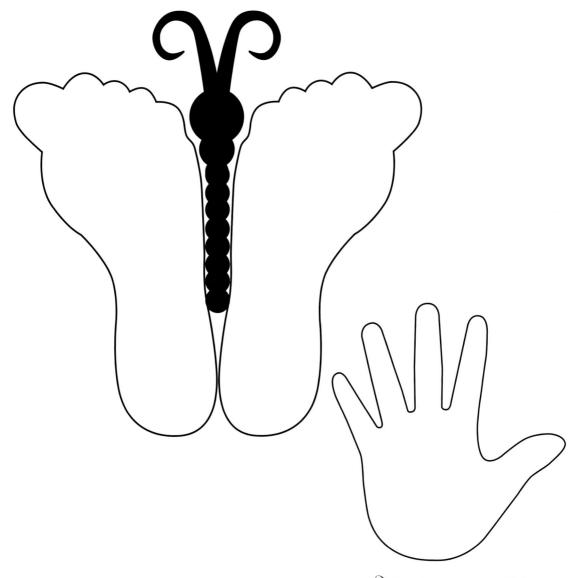

Templates for Hands and Feet Tea—117

NOTCH AND INSERT STRIP FOR STAND

CUT A PIECE OF STURDY PAPER FOR BEAR STAND

CUT A PIECE OF STURDY PAPER FOR BEAR STAND

Tools

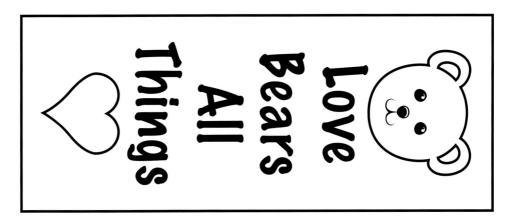

Love Bears All Things

Bobbie Wolgemuth

A love for children and enthusiasm for music, art, and literature have led Bobbie Wolgemuth to help young people find beauty and purpose in everyday celebrations. Her passion for Christ and her vision for families have given her the opportunity to teach Bible studies, open her home to neighbors, and sing hymns with children of all ages.

With a background in elementary education and music, she loves to bring spiritual truths to life in creative ways. Bobbie is the author or coauthor of eleven books, including the Gold Medallion–winning bestseller *Hymns for a Kid's Heart* (four volumes), with Joni Eareckson Tada. Her other books include *With Love from Mom*, The Great Hymns of Our Faith series (four volumes with Joni Eareckson Tada, Dr. John MacArthur, and her husband, Robert), *The Most Important Year in a Woman's Life: What Every Bride Needs to Know* (with Susan DeVries), and *How to Lead Your Child to Christ* (with her husband, Robert).

Bobbie has been a frequent guest on the *Focus on the Family* radio broadcast and *Family Life Today* on such topics as motherhood, marriage, and music.

Over the past several years, Bobbie has led retreats for young mothers, enjoyed prayer and encouragement in a Bible study group for moms, and regularly hosted a steady stream of children at her home for tea parties with a purpose.

Bobbie attended Taylor University and Trinity University. She has been married to Robert since 1970 and has two married daughters, Missy Schrader and Julie Tassy. Bobbie loves to have tea parties with her grandchildren Abby, Luke, and Isaac Schrader and Harper and Ella Tassy. She also enjoys painting, playing the piano, and collecting antique hymn books.

Please send us pictures of your favorite tea parties. For new ideas and to share yours, visit our website at www.teapartieswithapurpose.com.